How To Become A Successful Student

From A-Z

Shawn M. McBride

How To Become A Successful Student From A-Z
Copyright © 2015 by Shawn M. McBride

All rights reserved. No part of this book may be reproduced or transmitted in any form or by any means without written permission from the author.

ISBN-13:
978-1505437607

ISBN-10:
1505437601

Dedication

This book is dedicated to the six remarkable and outstanding teachers from my formative grade school years that laid a solid and strong foundation that has enabled me to become a lifelong learner.

Ms. Shuman 1st Grade Teacher
Mrs. Spears 2nd Grade Teacher
Mrs. Brody 3rd Grade Teacher
Mrs. Landerfield 4th Grade Teacher
Mr. Fisher 5th Grade Teacher
Mr. Green 6th Grade Teacher

TABLE OF CONTENTS

A IS FOR ATTITUDE	7
B IS FOR BELIEFS	10
C IS FOR COURAGE	13
D IS FOR DILIGENCE	15
E IS FOR ENDURANCE	17
F IS FOR FOCUS	20
G IS FOR GOALS	22
H IS FOR HEALTH	25
I IS FOR INTEGRITY	28
J IS FOR JUSTICE	30
K IS FOR KINDNESS	32
L IS FOR LEARNING	34
M IS FOR MOTIVATION	36
N IS FOR NAVIGATION	38
O IS FOR ORGANIZATION	40
P IS FOR PURPOSE	42
Q IS FOR QUESTIONING	44
R IS FOR RESILIENCE	46

S IS FOR STRENGTHS	48
U IS FOR UNIFICATION	52
V IS FOR VALUES	54
W IS FOR WISDOM	56
X IS FOR X-RAY VISION	57
Y IS FOR YIELDING	58
Z IS FOR ZEAL	60

Introduction

American children spend at least 16-20 years of their lives receiving formal education. How To Become a Successful Student enlightens young people with 26 practical and easy-to-remember principles from A-Z that will help them excel in this journey. Each principle, such as the power of ATTITUDE, the importance of setting GOALS, staying ORGANIZED and becoming RESILIENT, is clearly defined and explained in a way that young people can understand and relate to. Each principle is followed by an action step and provides valuable knowledge to help each student achieve SUCCESS in the classroom and beyond the school doors.

About The Author

Shawn McBride is an author and phenomenal national youth motivational speaker who presents top-quality messages at public, private and alternative schools. Born in Washington DC, McBride has spoken to over half a million young people across the United States. He is highly qualified and recognized as a dynamic communicator and advocate for students from elementary school through college. McBride's messages transform the attitudes and aspirations of students. His teachings motivate students to excel in school and life. He encourages students to pursue academic achievement and inspires them to believe that they can accomplish their dreams. McBride is keenly aware of the needs of today's young people and how to articulate information and principles in a way they can learn while laughing.

A is for Attitude

Attitude is a choice.

Two people can be in the same place, standing side by side, doing the same thing, and have two very different experiences. The difference is their attitude about the situation. The way we view a situation changes everything. Our mind is a very powerful tool.

Let's look at this example.

Two friends, Jack and Todd, go to the movies on a Friday night. Jack goes to the movies all the time. His parents give him the money freely, every time he asks. He is able to walk the mall, watch a movie, and order popcorn whenever he wants.

On the other hand, Todd's family doesn't have the money to give him. Todd works a part-time job at a restaurant for spending money. Because of his work schedule, he usually has to spend his free time catching up on homework. His job takes up a lot of his time. So, going to the movies on a Friday night is kind of a big deal for Todd.

Todd even lets Jack pick the movie. But, when the movie is over and the empty popcorn tubs are thrown away, Todd and Jack leave the theater with different reactions. Funny thing is, Jack starts complaining. He thinks the movie was boring; a let-down;

a waste of time. Todd is surprised since he thought the movie was awesome. He was on the edge of his seat.

What do you think is the difference between Jack and Todd's attitude?

Todd has a grateful attitude. Jack does not, but he can turn it around if he makes the right choice. The world looks different when we have a grateful attitude. Colors seem brighter. We notice the little things. We are grateful for the little things. When it comes down to it, life is all about the little moments. Having gratitude gives us a rich and meaningful life. The people around us feel appreciated.

A person with a positive attitude looks for the good. And they are grateful when they find it. Be a detective looking for the good.

Everyone wins.

Todd goes home having enjoyed the night. Jack goes home feeling disappointed and looking for something else that seems more fulfilling.

Same movie but very different experiences. It's all about attitude.

Take Action

Keep a gratitude journal. At the end of every day, jot down three things you are grateful for. They can be big or small. Personal, academic, social, etc. Something that stuck out to you through the day.

Begin the practice now.

Take out a piece of paper and write out three things you are grateful for today. If you feel inspired, share them with the people who matter most.

B is for Beliefs

All of us have beliefs. These beliefs define who we are. Beliefs are the persistent thoughts swirling around inside of our heads. They guide what we do and don't do.

Where do they come from?

We get our beliefs from our parents, family members, friends, friends' families, education, organizations, and our life experiences. They are such a part of us that we often forget they are there.

Why are they important?

It's important to examine our beliefs because they play a huge part in our actions. They encompass 3 main areas:

- Beliefs about ourselves.
- Beliefs about the world around us.
- Beliefs about our future.

We will feel good and act according to our goals if our beliefs about ourselves, the world and our futures are positive. If our beliefs about life are negative, we will have a bleak vision of ourselves, other and our future. The world looks very different depending on our beliefs.

So, what can you do about it?

1. **Become a belief detective.**

Think back to something that happened this past week that made you upset. Ask yourself, what was I thinking about myself, others and my future? If you can, jot these thoughts down.

There they are, your beliefs. Chances are, these beliefs come up often when you are upset.

Example: Everyone else is better than me.

2. **Challenge your beliefs.**

Check these thoughts for accuracy. We often keep beliefs in our minds even if they are not true. Just like us, our minds get into bad habits.

Ask yourself, are they true? Are they accurate? Are they helpful? Should I keep them?

Example: Is it really true that everyone else is better than me?

3. **Replace your beliefs.**

Once you see these unhelpful beliefs on paper, you may realize they are neither true nor helpful. So, it's time to intentionally change them. If you don't, they may stick around. Replace them with something realistic and believable. Just telling yourself you're the smartest person in the whole world will probably not help because you won't be able to believe it. Come up with something real.

Example:

I am neither the smartest nor the dumbest person here. I have something unique to offer. Something would be missing without my contribution.

Take Action

Take some time to compete this activity now. Choose an activating situation that happened this past week and become a belief detective.

C is for Courage

Courage as the ability to do something that you know is difficult or dangerous.

This life requires us to be courageous. Success goes hand in hand with courage. Without courage, we opt out of experiences because they scare us. The trick is to acknowledge that you're scared and push through to the end.

Many situations in this life are scary. But, the truth is, we have to go through them. It's way easier to muscle through with courage. The alternative is to miss out.

Let's look at Jen's story of courage.

Jen is a junior in high school. Since she was a little girl, Jen has dealt with a learning disability. She struggles with assignments that seem easy for her classmates. Books take her much longer to read. It doesn't seem fair.

It would be easy for her to complain.

But, Jen has courage. Jen wants to get into college. She wants to go become an attorney. Her family believes in her. They help her access the learning tools she needs to support her learning.

Her grades are high.

What's interesting about this story? Believe it or not, most people don't know Jen has a disability. It takes her a lot of courage to persevere in the face of her disability. She chooses not to complain and doesn't ask for sympathy. While there are times she leans into the compassionate arms of her family, Jen continues to push forward towards her goals.

Jen wins.

Being courageous take practice, just like physical exercise, and you will get better and better at it. The first courageous step we take is often the most difficult. Just like the first day of a new workout routine, building courage is tough.

There are all different kinds of courage. Courage requires us to face fear and act anyway. It requires us to follow our hearts and endure challenges.

We confront what we are afraid of and conquer it.

Take Action

Decide this week to stand up for something right. Something will come up that will require you to stand up for what you know is fair and just. Stand up for someone, speak up, do the right thing. Wait for an opportunity and then seize it.

D is for Diligence

Diligence is about commitment. Constant and earnest effort. Diligence applies to personal goals, school assignments, work requirements and relationships.

How do we get to our goals?

Big accomplishments in life are a compilation of small choices. Following through in small, incremental steps. It's not one day, or one choice. Those daily decisions help us reach our goals.

We continue to act even when the finish line is nowhere in sight.

Large changes happen slowly. The change usually doesn't last if we leap into something too quickly. It requires discipline and devotion.

Let's look at an example.

If someone wants to get into better physical shape, it requires minute-by-minute choices. They can't just decide to lose weight and accomplish it in one day. It requires daily decisions. Eating the right foods, avoiding junk food, finding ways to be more active. A walk around the block every day is better than one 10-minute sprint.

If you want to improve your grades, it doesn't mean having 1 meeting with your teacher or writing one awesome essay.

What does it take?

Improving your grades requires daily discipline. Being diligent about your grades means practicing the daily discipline of organization, completing assignments, finishing reading and turning in your work on time. Every time.

If you slip up, you restart. Simple.

We build confidence in ourselves when we choose to live this way. We realize we are capable of making good decisions, and following through with each positive choice we make. We are proud of ourselves when we follow through.

Can you remember a time when you were proud of yourself for completing a task?

Practice being diligent.

Take Action

Think of one of your life goals today. It may be academic, physical, social or personal. Ask yourself what steps you can begin making today to reach that goal. Remember to think small and reachable. This may require you to break your goal down into smaller milestones. Think through it and begin acting on your decision today.

E is for Endurance

What do you think of when you hear the word endurance? Maybe you think of a runner in a marathon. What makes that runner finish the race?

They choose to continue running despite feeling mentally and physically tired. They continue to place one foot in front of the other. They continue moving forward.

Can you think of a time when you pushed through something even though you were tired or stressed out?

We might not feel like doing something. We're tired. We're overwhelmed. Our favorite show is coming on. Our iPod just finished charging. Our friend calls to chat.

What sets successful people apart from everyone else is their ability to endure making choices that help them reach their goal.

If everyone stopped when they were tired or stressed, many would not achieve the success they are capable of. They would not finish the race. And what a shame that would be!

Have you heard about someone who was so close to finishing something and suddenly stopped?

There are countless tales of people with six credits left to finish their bachelor's degree, one payment away from paying off a credit card, one phone call away from reconnecting with an old friend, one stellar assignment away from a nailing down a better GPA.

Don't let this happen to you.

Let's take a look at Ryan's story.

Ryan set a goal at the beginning of his senior year to finally conquer his difficulty with math. He worked at it all year. He brainstormed with his teachers, hired a tutor, did extra work, set aside ample homework time, and studied before each quiz and test.

Then, it was close to the end of the year. Friends were meeting up at the beach every week for volleyball. Other students were cutting classes. The last thing anybody was doing was studying for a test. Most of the students had heard back from their colleges of choice. What did it matter?

What matters is that Ryan set a goal for himself and he chose to stick with it. That meant missing out on volleyball and choosing not to cut class. Despite some teasing from friends, he chose to study instead.

He ended up getting the highest grade in his class.

Sometimes we think people who succeed in life must have some amazing ability or special fortune. The truth is that those who achieve success in this life choose to press on through adversity. Even when they feel like giving up.

Can you think of someone in your life who made the choice to endure, despite hardships?

Take Action

Take some time to call this person. Tell them why you admire them and invite them to share what it took to endure the hardship they faced.

F is for Focus

Imagine it's a beautiful, fall day. The leaves haven't fallen yet and everything is full of vibrant color. A family is enjoying a spontaneous photo session with a beach landscape in the background. Even though you are sitting a distance away, you can tell it would be a great shot.

Maybe even good enough to frame and hang.

One thing stands in the way of that picture being great: focus.

Without focus, the picture is blurry. You can't make out the details.

It's the same principle in life. Everything is blurry and our path is unclear when we don't have the focus,. Focus helps us set our direction and determine the steps.

How do we determine our focus? We set clear, definable goals. How do we set clear goals? We dig deep.

Let's say someone has a goal to make a lot of money. Is that a clear goal? Would it be easy to create action steps towards that goal? No.

We have to dig deeper.

We have to ask ourselves why something is important to us. Why is it important to make a lot of money? What we may find is there are dreams hidden underneath that lofty endeavor. We may crave security, freedom and the ability to be generous with others.

Think about your life goals. Is it to make a lot of money, fall in love or have a family? Think about what is motivating you to achieve your goals. Paint a clear picture about what encompasses your goal.

Once you establish a goal, ask yourself why it is important. Continue to peel the layers back until you've uncovered the root purpose.

This is where you will find clarity and direction.

Take Action

Write down a goal and write down why it is important. Then, answer it again. And again.

1. My Goal
2. Why is that important?
3. Why is that important?
4. Why is that important?

G Is For Goals

There is one thing that is set long before an accomplishment is reached: a goal. A goal must be set before plans can be made and dreams can have room to grow. Without a goal, the journey towards success is cloudy, like walking along a foggy path, hands stretched out reaching for clarity. You have a sense you're going the right way, but unsure whether or not you've taken the right steps. We can all get discouraged along the way to our dreams on a path without goals.

Long and Short Term Goals

It's important to set both small and large goals, both in the long and short term. The large goals are the big dreams for our lives, while the small goals represent milestones reached on the way to our larger vision.

Think of it this way. Joe wants to be accepted to college. Joe has to set smaller, short-term goals along the way in order to accomplish this dream. Perhaps his short-term goals may be keeping up his GPA, prepping for the SAT's and registering for several extracurricular activities. Meeting these marks along the way provide Joe with passion and encouragement.

SMART Goals

Let's talk about setting "SMART" goals.

"SMART" goals meet the following qualifications:
- **Specific**

    Goals need to be specific and clearly defined. If your goal is simply "to be happy," it is not specific enough. Rather, it could be something like, "get accepted to three of my choice colleges."

- **Measurable**

    How will you know when you've achieved your goal? You must set a measurable goal. "Happiness" alone is not a measurable goal. However, "spend more time doing leisurely activities" and "devote more time with close friends" are measurable goals.

- **Attainable**

    Ask yourself, is this goal attainable? You will get discouraged and likely veer off the route if you set a goal you can't possibly attain. For example, "I will never ever eat sugar again," is not an attainable goal, because it is too extreme and limiting for most people.

- **Realistic**

    Is your goal realistic? Do you have a reasonable chance to achieve your goal? We are more likely to enjoy success when we set realistic goals,.

- **Timely**

Goals should be able to be accomplished at some reasonable time in the future. You may get discouraged by not seeing immediate results if you say you want to be a millionaire by the time you are 75-years-old. It's better to set a timely goal that you're more likely to meet.

Take Action

Write down one bigger, long-term goal that you want to achieve. Now write down three smaller, short-term goals that are realistic to achieve in the next month and will move you forward to reaching your long-term goal.

H is for Health

Ever try to do something when you are hungry or tired? It's difficult to stay on task when we don't feel great. Our health is connected to everything we do.

Let's look at the main aspects of our health that are within our control:

- Nutrition
- Exercise
- Adequate sleep

Nutrition

Food is fuel for our bodies.

Our bodies will not function as intended if our fuel is made up of fast food and candy bars. Sugar and simple carbohydrates may give us a momentary boost, but over a few hours will leave us sluggish and craving more junk food.

Better to fuel up with healthy proteins, complex carbohydrates, and vegetables that will power us through our day.

Do some research and find a nutrition regimen that will work for you and your family. Keep your body full and focused.

Exercise

Exercise is for everyone regardless of whether you consider yourself an athlete. It floods our brains with endorphins, which leave us feeling positive and focused.

Ask a friend or family member to take a walk in your neighborhood, play fetch with your dog, get up off the coach. Use opportunities to take the stairs, walk a little further to get where you're going. Do some jumping jacks.

Think about adding activity in throughout your day.

Sleep

Think you can go with only a few hours of sleep? Think again.

You are still growing and you will be for a while. Your body and brain need rest.

Limit the use of electronics before bed. There's nothing sleep-inducing about a glaring television screen. Try to put away your phone, power down your tablet and shut off the television 30 minutes before you close your eyes to get your brain in sleep-mode.

Don't eat a big meal before bed.

Create a nighttime ritual for yourself. Maybe it's a bath, some relaxing music or your favorite book. Whatever it is, stick to it and enjoy the benefits of a good night's sleep. You'll be even more productive tomorrow.

Take Action

Commit to taking good care of yourself. Eat wholesome, nourishing foods, fit physical activity into your day and make sure you get restful sleep.

I is for Integrity

Do you do what's right even if no one is looking?

Having integrity means that we act consistently based on our values regardless of the situation. We always do what we believe is right.

Ever feel that sharp pang in your chest when you know you're not doing the right thing?

The small voice you keep ignoring will become smaller and smaller if you keep writing it off. It's important to nurture integrity by listening to that small voice.

John and his sister, Beth, got into an argument. Beth told John she was going to text their dad about it while he was at work. John was furious. He couldn't stand when Beth tattle-tailed on him. He felt they were too old for all that nonsense. He saw her grab her cell phone and walk outside.

Later that afternoon, John saw his sister's phone sitting on the kitchen table. She was not around. Here was his chance.

He was so curious about what she wrote to their dad. All he had to do was pick up the phone and view her messages.

Then came the pang. He knew he shouldn't look at her phone. Even though he didn't like what she had done, he knew it wasn't right to violate her privacy. He wouldn't want someone doing that to him.

He avoided picking up the phone and walked away.

What do you think about John's choice?

As gratifying as it may have been in the moment, looking through his sister's phone would have been wrong. He would have violated her privacy. It would have been easy to do, and no one would have known.

Integrity is about making the right choice, regardless of reward. It's what we do when no one is looking.

We can act with integrity when we are clear about what is important to us. Privacy is important to John, so violating his sister's privacy was not going to happen.

Figure out what your values are and stick to them.

Take Action

Talk inventory of your friendships. Do you surround yourself with people who have integrity? Think of a friend who displays honesty and integrity. Find time today to talk about integrity with them.

J is for Justice

There are certain rights that everyone should be able to enjoy. Access to food, water, shelter, education and work. The benefits of kindness, compassion, dignity and respect.

Does it bother you that there are people who do not have the opportunity to enjoy these rights?

Sometimes it takes a big experience to realize how unfair this world can be to people.

Jake lives a comfortable life. His mom and dad both have good jobs. They live in a large house. Jake even got a brand new car for his 17th birthday.

He doesn't know what it's like to be poor, let alone hungry.

For Christmas one year, his parents decide to take the family to a local soup kitchen.

Jake is initially annoyed that he and his family won't enjoy their typical Christmas morning routine of homemade cinnamon rolls, hot chocolate and unwrapping presents all morning. His attitude shifts when they walk into the soup kitchen. He sees countless families, sitting closely together, enjoying their meals and laughing. They don't have gourmet kitchens and presents under their Christmas trees.

It's the first time Jake truly realizes that some people are not as fortunate as him.

He eagerly puts on an apron and follows instructions. He is more grateful than ever before.

He is learning about justice.

Christine enjoys helping out at the nursing home where her mom works. She believes the residents deserve companionship and laughter. Christine takes on the task of visiting with each patient each week.

She has been given a life full of love and joy, and feels it only right to pass it along. She has learned that meeting others' needs feeds her as well.

She seeks justice and does what is right.

Take Action

Look for an opportunity to provide for someone's need over the next few days. It may be a physical need or an emotional need. Maybe it's an encouraging word, or maybe it's giving your snack to someone who often goes without food.

K is for Kindness

Kindness is an *active* expression of love because it involves an action. If you say you're a kind person, it's because you *do* kind things. Notice the verb?

Being kind means acting in helpful and compassionate ways for the benefit of others. It is a deliberate action.

Has anyone ever shown kindness to you?

Lately, there has been a lot of talk about random acts of kindness. You probably have already heard of this expression. A random act of kindness is a kind action for someone else that is random, anonymous and unrewarded.

Have you ever done a random act of kindness?

Look at these examples of kindness:

- Saying something nice about someone else
- Being friendly to someone you don't usually talk to
- Being polite on social media
- Defending someone
- Showing appreciation to your parents or siblings
- Sharing something you have
- Doing chores around the house
- Befriending someone who seems lonely

- Thanking a teacher
- Giving a hug
- Stopping a negative conversation

Are you coming up with any other ideas of kind acts?

I bet you are. Kindness is contagious. It fuels our hearts to do good things for others. It is better to give than to receive.

Take Action

Do an act of service for someone free of charge. Maybe it's washing someone's car, offering to babysit, cleaning someone's house or mowing a lawn. Think up something and do it.

L is for Learning

What comes to mind when you think of the word learning? Do you think of school, textbooks, papers and exams?

Learning is a lifelong adventure beyond classrooms and books.

You will always be learning believe it or not. Every day presents us with new information.

Part of being successful is never losing your appetite for learning. Successful people are like sponges of knowledge. They can't get enough information. Feed your curiosity. If something triggers your interest, research it. If you want to know something about someone, ask them. Tell others about what you've found and inspire them.

Below are some benefits of a love for learning:

- Ability to adapt and change
- Desire to change the world around us
- Chance to inspire others
- Close relationships
- Regular inspiration

There is always something new to explore when we love to learn. This keeps life exciting. We all need excitement. People enjoy being around passionate people. Everyone longs to be inspired. Be a part of that.

Ways to learn outside of the classroom:

- Interesting blogs about topics you enjoy
- Search engines
- The great outdoors
- Friends, neighbors
- Grandparents
- Books
- Documentaries
- Local lectures

People have so much to offer. Get to know your grandparents, aunts and uncles. Ask them about what they do. Learn about their jobs, hobbies and life experiences. You will learn something new and they will get a chance to share their life with you.

Take Action

Learn something new right now. Call up someone you respect and ask them about their life. Keep asking questions until you learn something new. Ask them for details.

M is for Motivation

What would you do if you weren't afraid?

Simply put, motivation is the desire to do something. It is the opposite of laziness. It is not stopped by fear.

What motivates you?

We are all motivated by internal and external rewards. External rewards are things like praise, honor, gifts, money and free time. But the most lasting and inspiring rewards are those that are internal.

Examples of internal rewards:

- Knowing you did something meaningful and important
- Achieving success in a difficult task
- Realizing you overcame the odds
- Believing you helped someone else

We all long to be remembered for doing things that were meaningful and good. Usually these motivators are behind every goal that we set, if we look hard enough.

Ever feel unmotivated?

There are things you can do to increase your level of motivation.

Here are some ideas to boost your motivation:

- Celebrate your wins, big and small
- Set goals and enjoy your milestone successes
- Believe your dreams will come true
- Do some work toward your goals each day

Practice these and you will find you not only motivate yourself, but you motivate others, too. That's pretty cool.

Take Action

Think about a dream you have for your life. Write about a day in your life once you have achieved that dream.

N is for Navigation

Maps, roads, guides, milestones, reference points, signs. These days, people rely on technology to get where they are going. As you move forward in life, you will need to rely on similar principles to achieve success.

Who are your guides?

Guides help us navigate unknown trails. Guides can be our parents, grandparents, siblings, teachers, leaders, counselors and others we meet along the path. They may not have all of the answers, but they've been down the path before and have a lot of valuable information to share. We shouldn't be afraid to ask them for their guidance.
Humility is key.

How do we get a roadmap?

There are many people in our lives we can consult about laying out our roadmap. I wouldn't suggest doing that alone. Part of setting up a roadmap is knowing your destination, milestones, resting places, stops along the way and potential detours. Ask for help when you design your roadmap and make room for future changes. It is a working document, which means it will be modified and updated often.

What about detours?

Sometimes, we are walking in a certain direction, feeling confident in our steps, and all of a sudden we are faced with a detour sign. Things seem to be moving along perfectly, according to the plan, when life throws us a curveball. It's okay. It's important to remember that this happens to the best of us. Everyone has encountered a detour on the road to success. Road flooded, broken signs or bad advice.

The trick is to stay on the course.

Take Action

Identify five trail guides in your life. Write down their names and how they help you navigate your path.

O is for Organization

Ever sit down to complete an assignment for school only to realize something you needed was missing? Forgot a textbook or left the assignment in your locker?

Ever get to school, thinking the day is going smoothly, only to learn that the five-page essay you thought was due the following week was actually due that day?

Frustrating, right?

Being organized is a relief. We cannot do productive work unless we are organized. We must organize our belongings, time and priorities.

It's nice to know where things are. That favorite t-shirt? Bottom right drawer. Your science notebook? Backpack. Your work schedule? Under a magnet on the fridge.

Create a place for everything and keep everything in its place. There will be less time searching and more time being productive. The more time there will be for having fun the more productive and efficient you are with your time.

Keeping your time organized is equally as important.

Time slips away if we don't plan our days out. We need to be deliberate about scheduling. If you know you want to go out with friends Friday night, it's important to schedule your week out accordingly.

Use a planner. Write things in it.

Document everything: assignments, meetings, family time and friend time. Track homework assignments and extracurricular activities. Cross things off as you complete them.

You will feel good about yourself when you look at what you have accomplished. It's pretty amazing what you can do in one week. It builds self-esteem.

Organize your priorities.

Make a to-do list every day. Jot down what needs to be done and then number the items by importance. Have to study for two quizzes and write an essay? Determine what will take the most time, what needs to be done first and how you can break it down into more manageable parts.

Take Action

Start making daily to-do lists if you're not already doing it. They can be written on anything: a fancy notepad, a school notebook, an app or a napkin. It doesn't matter. Just write down your daily tasks (academic, personal, etc.) and cross things off as you accomplish them.

P is for Purpose

Why are you doing what you do? Do you know?

You may not stay the course if you're not sure.

It's critical to have a purpose for everything you do. So many people aimlessly work, running towards a goal. It may be a goal others have set for them.

You will eventually lose your footing if you're chasing after someone else's dream.

You can tell when someone is living with purpose. They have fun and relax with friends. There is a greater purpose behind everything they do. A reason.

Claire has a busy schedule. She shines academically. She plays soccer, works part-time at the mall, volunteers as a receptionist at the hospital and makes time to be silly with friends.

Her friends wonder where all her energy comes from. They secretly envy her ability to get it all done.

What makes Claire different?

Claire has a purpose. She wants to make her family proud. She does everything purposefully in order to grow her sense of self-worth. There's a purpose grander than receiving good grades or a paycheck.

Do you know anyone who has purpose?

It could be for their family, future career or a dream. They may want to make their parents proud, support a family one day or know they came up with something great. They may want to change their corner of the world.

How can you figure out what your purpose is?

Take Action

Create a dream board. Take a pile of magazines and photos and rip out the ones that speak to you. Pick out pictures that say something about the life you want. Paste them onto a board and take a step back. What have you created? Why is it important? Where are you headed?

Q is for Questioning

There are no dumb questions. Has anyone ever said that to you?

Well, it's true.

Questioning leads us to greater knowledge. It helps us clarify our thoughts. We learn through asking questions.

Ever feel embarrassed about asking a question?

The question we ask may be the one someone near us needed to ask, but didn't. Use your boldness and be their voice.

Curious people get further in life. They ask questions and research information. They are always learning and growing. They desire more knowledge.

Still feel silly asking more questions?

It's okay to ask for more details when you are uncomfortable. There are times you may need to ask for clearer directions on an assignment. Chances are, your classmates were wondering the same thing.

Take Action

Write down two questions about something you feel confused about or wanted to ask but didn't. Find the courage and go to the person you know who has the answers.

R is for Resilience

Facing difficult situations and loss is part of life. Inevitably, you will face times in life that knock you off your feet. Will you be able to get back up? Do you have what it takes?

Resilience is the ability to bounce back after facing a hardship. It is the capacity to change and alter our plan in order to bounce back and get back up in the face of difficulty.

Lately, scientists have done a lot of research on resilience. They've studied adults, children and adolescents.

What did they find?

- Some people are more resilient than others
- Factors that influence resilience
- People can improve their capacity for resilience

Some people are naturally more resilient than others. They bounce back again and again in the face of adversity despite their circumstances.

The good news is that you can actually improve their resilience over time. You can grow their ability to bounce back from tough situations if you believe you are resilient and don't fall into a victim mindset.

Factors that strengthen our resilience:

- Maintaining meaningful relationships
- Developing positive self-esteem
- Having the skills to handle troubling emotions
    - Stress, anger, frustration
- Possessing problem-solving skills
- Being a good communicator
- Feeling a sense of control over your life
- Accessing help when needed
- Feeling like you are doing something meaningful or larger than yourself
- Believing you are resilient

Take Action

Take a look at your level of resilience. Remember a time you bounced back after a difficult situation? Write about how you did it. You build your ability to be able to act the same way again. when you deliberately think this way. It's in you.

S is for Strengths

Do you know your strengths and weaknesses?

We all have strengths and weakness. Attributes that build us up and qualities that could use some work. Which do you choose to focus on?

We are all uniquely gifted. Take a look at the list below and choose some strengths that you have.
  Adventurous
  Caring
  Motivated
  Spontaneous
  Courageous
  Warm
  Open minded
Passionate
Curious
Diligent
Honest
Realistic
Daring
Enduring

  Creative

Friendly

Fun
Generous
Hard working
Honorable
Inspiring
Joyful

Think about the strengths that make you different from others. What's interesting about our biggest strengths is that sometimes they come easily to us. This can give us the idea that everyone shares the same strengths. Truth is, your strengths are unique.

It is your responsibility to contribute your strengths to the world.

You will rob yourself and the world of the amazing gifts you have to offer if you choose to only focus on your weaknesses.

Take Action

Look over the strengths list above. Choose the top three qualities you possess. Feel free to add a word if you don't see it. Brainstorm and list several ways those strengths will benefit the world.

T is for Teamwork

Sometimes, working on a team can be hard work. Have you ever been frustrated while working on a team?

Successful teams require thoughtful planning. Consider these five tips the next time you work on a team:

1. Leadership

Every team needs a leader. Why not you? This person's responsibility is to motivate, inspire and keep the team organized and on task. Ideally, this is achieved with humility and mutual respect.

2. Clear Direction

It's important to define the goals and tasks of the group. Is it clear what the team is supposed to accomplish? Work together to figure out the tasks and break them down into workable projects. Then, make sure each group member understands the goals.

3. Responsibility

The team can assign team members different tasks now that the goals are defined. Make each person responsible for part of the project. It is not fair for one person to complete most of the work nor is it the best use of the team. Teams can often produce better work collectively than one person alone.

4. Feedback

It's important for the group to continue to communicate and provide each other with updates about progress once tasks are defined. A breakdown in communication will lead to a disconnected team.

5. Diversity

Celebrate and capitalize on what makes each team member different. If someone is better at public speaking then someone else, assign them to present. Be a part of making sure people's strengths are utilized efficiently.

Take Action

Practice being a leader the next time you are on a team. Look out for diversity in your teammates and capitalize on their strengths. Foster communication. Motivate!

U is for Unification

Be a peacemaker. Seek to bring people together. Encourage relationships. The power to do this is within you.

Have you ever sat idly by while someone was ridiculed or left out of a group? Have you ever intervened?

Chris is the captain of his baseball team and he sat with a bunch of his teammates after practice one afternoon. They were all talking about another teammate, Jay, who had to borrow used equipment for the season. Chris was uncomfortable as he listened to them tease Jay, but he did nothing. He chuckled along with the group.

What could Chris have done differently to unify the group?

Chris could have spoken up and gently reminded the team that Jay's parents had just gotten divorced and didn't have a lot of money. The team probably would have respected what Chris had to say and given Jay a break.

How would this have impacted the team?

Jay would have felt as though he was more valuable to the group. His teammates would have felt good about themselves for including Jay and focusing on his true talent, not the used mitt.

People don't typically like leaving others out deep down. Many people follow the pack and don't speak up against injustice.

Be the one that speaks up.

Take Action

Look for an opportunity to bring people together. Wait for the chance to unite friends. It will happen and you will be ready to act.

V is for Values

Stick to your values. We enjoy living an authentic, happy life when we live every day according to our values. This is how to be true to yourself and what you believe in.

Our values guide how we spend our time, the people we associate with and what our futures will look like.

Time is a limited resource. This day will pass regardless of what we do with it. Time will simply pass by if we are not deliberate about what we do with our time, it will simply go away.

Life is much more meaningful when we do things we value every day. Life will feel full and happy when you fill your time with meaningful pursuits.

Think about your values. Take a look at the list below.

    Relationships
    Achievement
    Connection
    Preservation
    Conservation
    Inspiration
    Compassion
    Integrity
    Generosity

Love
Wealth
Peace

These are just a few examples of values. Can you think of more? Which are the most valuable to you?

Take Action

Ask yourself: What is most important to me? Why? What steps are you taking to show that love, generosity or other attributes take priority in your life?

W is for Wisdom

Life experiences grow wisdom. We have the opportunity to gain wisdom every day. We still have a lot of wisdom we need to gain when we are young. People who have traveled in this life longer have more insight, common sense, life experiences and lessons they have learned.

Where do we find wisdom?

Well, it can't be purchased at a store and ordered online. There are two primary ways we gain wisdom.

1. Life experiences
2. The wisdom of others

We want more of it once we see the true value of wisdom. Truth is, it takes time.

The first secret is to simply appreciate wisdom.

Listen when people talk. Learn from their stories. Ask questions. Listen to their secrets.

Take Action

Call a family member today and ask them their secrets for living a successful life.

X is for X-Ray Vision

X-ray vision is the ability to see through something. To look beyond the surface and be able to analyze what is going on underneath.

Bonnie says she's fine. Her family is going through a tough time. Her dad lost his job and her parents are fighting a lot. They are talking about splitting up. She's the oldest and worries about her two younger brothers.

Her friends notice she seems distant and sad. They ask her how she is doing. They ask her what's wrong. She always says she's fine.

Luckily, her friend Paula has x-ray vision. Paula sees beyond Bonnie's weak smile. She shares her concerns with Bonnie. Bonnie feels relieved that someone saw through her façade.

Have you ever used x-ray vision?

Take Action

Look for a situation that requires x-ray vision and be brave enough to use it.

Y is for Yielding

Jason knows he is smart. He always knows the answer and sticks up his hand when a teacher asks a question in class. He blurts out the answer when his class plays a trivia game. He corrects his friends on the rules when they play kickball. The rules are the rules.

What is Jason doing wrong?

He is not yielding to others. He is not giving his classmates the chance to contribute. He is placing rules above friendships.

Kara is working on a team project with her classmates. They are brainstorming ideas for the topic of their project. People are throwing ideas out excitedly. The team's morale is strong. Kara grows impatient and stops the brainstorming. She decides on the topic and instructs the group to agree.

What could be the consequences of Kara not yielding?

Kara's team may grow discouraged and not be excited about their project. The team members will not feel as invested as they did in the beginning because they feel their opinions do not matter.

What would have happen if Kara had yielded to her teammates?

The group could have collaborated about the topic and chosen one they all could feel good about. Kara could have inserted her idea without bulldozing the group. Everyone could have been heard.

Truth is, everyone's contribution is valuable.

Take Action

Look for a chance to yield to someone today. Listen to what they have to say and see the value in their contribution.

Z is for Zeal

Zeal is a passion for life. Zeal is contagious. It's exciting.

Have you ever met someone passionate about something? What were they like? What did their passion do to you?

Being around a passionate person is inspiring. We feel more passionate after being around them. We have a renewed hunger for life.

What are you passionate about?

Frank loves to run. His dad instilled in him a love for running when he was a little kid. He plays all kinds of sports but especially loves track. He runs for fun with his dad whenever he has the chance. He runs for charities and community events.

His room is covered in posters about running. He talks about it all the time. He's inspired several of his friends and classmates to start running. One of his classmates, Jackie, used running to lose weight. Even several of his teachers have taken up running.

What if Frank had kept his zeal for running to himself?

There would be fewer runners in the world. Imagine all the people Frank will continue to inspire because of his zeal.

What are you zealous about? Do you share it or keep it to yourself?

Take Action

Figure out something you are zealous about and choose one person to share it with today.

Made in the USA
Columbia, SC
20 June 2018